11

Major Competitive Reality Shows:
Making the Band

Karen Schweitzer

Mason Crest Publishers
Philadelphia

Mason Crest Publishers
370 Reed Road
Broomall, PA 19008
www.masoncrest.com

CPSIA Compliance Information: Batch #060110-MCRS. For further information, contact Mason Crest Publishers at 1-866-MCP-Book

First printing
1 3 5 7 9 8 6 4 2

Library of Congress Cataloging-in-Publication Data

Schweitzer, Karen.
  Major competitive reality shows: Making the band / Karen Schweitzer.
    p. cm. — (Major competitive reality shows)
  Includes bibliographical references and index.
  ISBN 978-1-4222-1674-3 (hc)
  ISBN 978-1-4222-1937-9 (pb)
  1. Making the band (Television program)—Juvenile literature. 2. Popular music—Competitions—United States—Juvenile literature. I. Title.
  ML76.M35S39 2010
  791.45'72—dc22
                          2010019245

Photo credits: © American Broadcasting Companies, Inc.: 4, 8; AP/Wide World Photo: cover, 17, 23, 31, 32, 35; Getty Images: 18, 24, 40; used under license from Shutterstock, Inc.: 1, 6, 11, 14, 15, 27, 39, 43.

Contents

1

The members of O-Town included Jacob Underwood, Ashley Parker Angel, Erik-Michael Estrada, Trevor Penick, and Dan Miller. The formation of this band and its early career were documented in the original seasons of the reality show *Making the Band*.

Making a Boy Band

Reality-based TV shows are so common today that it's almost hard to imagine a time when the *genre* wasn't a staple of American television. Many people date the boom in reality programming to 2000. In May of that year, *Survivor* debuted on CBS to blockbuster ratings.

Two months earlier, however, ABC had premiered its own reality series. Like *Survivor*, it was a competition show. But its contestants, unlike those on the CBS show, weren't given a series of contrived tasks to perform. Rather, they had to demonstrate their vocal and dance skills, competing for the chance to become members of a boy band.

THE HISTORY OF BOY BANDS

The term *boy band* was coined in the 1990s, but all-male bands existed long before then. In the 1960s there were the Beatles, the Monkees, and the Jackson 5. In the 1970s, 1980s, and 1990s, all-male groups like New Edition and New Kids on the Block topped the music charts.

6 Making the Band

One of the best-known boy band managers in the 1990s was Lou Pearlman. Pearlman started out in the *aviation* business, but eventually decided he would rather be in the music business after one of his charter planes flew New Kids on the Block to several concerts.

"I got to see a New Kids on the Block concert. It was fantastic," Pearlman told the *Orlando Business Journal*. "With a young lady friend of mine, I decided what a trip it would be to get involved in this business. So we went ahead and put together the concept and got a group."

That group included Nick Carter, Howie Dorough, Brian Littrell, A. J. McLean, and Kevin Richardson. Together they were known as the Backstreet Boys. The group rose to stardom quickly and became one of the highest-selling male vocal groups of all time.

Inspired by the success of the Backstreet Boys, Pearlman helped form another group in 1995. Known as 'NSYNC, its members included Lance Bass, JC Chasez, Joey Fatone, Chris Kirkpatrick, and Justin Timberlake. Like the Backstreet Boys, 'NSYNC was wildly successful right from the start.

The Backstreet Boys were among the most popular musical groups of the late 1990s and early 2000s. The group sold more than 130 million albums. Their biggest hits included "I Want It That Way" and "Quit Playing Games (With My Heart)."

FROM CONCEPT TO REALITY

After seeing what Lou Pearlman had done with the Backstreet Boys and 'NSYNC, Ken Mok, vice president for development at MTV Productions, approached him about doing a television show documenting what it takes to make a boy band. The show would follow potential band members as they auditioned, went through vocal coaching, learned choreography, and recorded songs.

Pearlman agreed to work as the *executive producer* for the show, which would eventually be named *Making the Band*. The show was set to air on ABC in the spring of 2000. It would be the network's very first reality-based TV show.

THE FIRST SEASON

The producers of *Making the Band* held an open audition on November 6, 1999, to find members for the band. More than 1,800 aspiring musical artists showed up. Judges chose 25 talented hopefuls out of the group. They later narrowed the field to just eight guys.

Making the Band premiered on ABC on March 25, 2000. The first episode, along with every other episode in the season, began with the same spoken intro: "This series follows eight young performers as they compete for five positions in a new band. There are no actors, no scripts: just raw talent, a dream and cameras recording every step of the journey."

The eight young performers were Ashley Parker Angel, Bryan Chan, Erik-Michael Estrada, Ikaika Kahoano, Jacob Underwood, Michael Miller, Paul Martin, and

Fast Fact

The first season of *Making the Band* used the same production crew as MTV's popular reality show *The Real World*.

Trevor Penick. Cameras followed all of the boys as they spent seven hours each day dancing, singing, and getting to know each other.

More than 200 hours of tape were recorded every week. After watching all of the tape, the show's editors picked out what they considered to be the most exciting moments. These moments were then cut into a 22-minute episode.

Making the Band producer Lou Pearlman (center) poses with the first season finalists. Pearlman had already shown that he knew how create a successful group, having previously made the Backstreet Boys and 'NSYNC into stars.

Making the Band was popular right from the start. Viewers seemed to get caught up in the competition, and they tuned in to see what would happen next in the life of the band. The show was ranked number one in its time slot among viewers under the age of 49. It was especially popular among the under-18 crowd.

O-TOWN

Midway through the first season of *Making the Band,* three of the cast members (Bryan, Michael, and Paul) were eliminated. The remaining cast (Ashley, Erik, Ikaika, Jacob, and Trevor) were the chosen members of the new band, which would be called O-Town.

O-Town began recording its first album on camera. Early in the process, Ikaika chose to leave the show and the band to return home

Fast Fact

The name of the band, O-Town, was chosen in honor of Orlando, Florida.

to his family in Hawaii. The remaining band members were then left with the difficult task of finding a replacement for him. They eventually chose Dan Miller, one of the 25 who had emerged from the original auditions, to become the fifth member of O-Town. Together, the five members of the band played a concert for the MTV network during the final episode of the season.

MAKING THE BAND RETURNS

The second season of *Making the Band* premiered on the ABC network in April 2001. Cameras rolled as the band members heard their album's first single, "Liquid Dreams," on the radio for the first time.

"Liquid Dreams" was a huge success, reaching number one on the Billboard singles sales chart and peaking at number 10 on the Billboard

Hot 100 chart. The album's other singles achieved similar success. The biggest hit was "All or Nothing," which was nominated for Song of the Year at the 2001 Radio Music Awards.

Throughout the *Making the Band* season, the members of O-Town enjoyed their success. But they worked harder than ever—on camera and off—to prove that they were more than just TV personalities. They visited radio stations, began a nationwide tour, and hired new management to secure new opportunities in the music business.

THIRD SEASON

The second season of *Making the Band* was a huge hit among viewers between the ages of 12 and 24. The show's success on ABC did not go unnoticed by other television networks, especially MTV. The MTV network, which has always made an effort to appeal to the 12–24 crowd, decided to pick up the show from ABC.

The third season of *Making the Band* premiered on MTV on January 19, 2002. In the first episode, O-Town was invited to tour with Britney Spears. Subsequent episodes showed the guys getting to know each other better, fighting and later making up, participating in radio contests, and touring the world.

In the final episodes of season three, fans got to watch as O-Town worked on the group's second album. The band members became upset when a critic said they sounded manufactured and packaged. The guys decided the best thing they could do was work hard to show the critic—and everyone else—that they cared about their music.

THE END OF O-TOWN

O-Town's second album, *O2*, was released in November 2002, several months after the third season of *Making the Band* had ended. The guys

Lasting Success

Ashley Parker Angel got his first taste of musical success as a member of O-Town. But when the cameras stopped rolling and the band's career fizzled, life became very difficult for the young singer.

Ashley dreamed of launching a solo singing career. But he was forced to take low-paying jobs to support himself and his pregnant girlfriend, Tiffany Lynn. When MTV heard about Ashley's situation, the network wanted to make a show out of it. When MTV approached Ashley with a proposal to tell his story in another reality show, he was hesitant. Eventually, however, he agreed to go back in front of the cameras.

Ashley's new reality show, *There and Back*, premiered on MTV on January 9, 2006. Much of the show revolved around the making of his solo album, *Soundtrack to Your Life*. Ashley's album was released on May 16, 2006. It debuted at number five on the Billboard 200 albums chart.

After achieving musical success once more, Ashley decided to give acting a try. He signed on to play the lead in the award-winning musical *Hairspray*. Producers were so pleased with his performance that they extended his contract four times.

Ashley's latest projects include a voice-over appearance on Disney's *Handy Manny* and a movie role in *Wild Things: Foursome*.

Ashley Parker Angel was born the same day that the MTV network debuted: August 1, 1981.

had worked hard on the project and were pleased with the result. They were sure that the album would prove they were a legitimate music group with real talent. In an interview with *Billboard* magazine, band member Ashley Parker Angel explained why it was so important for them to put out a great record the second time around:

> I hated that the TV show stood for the fact that you could just add water and mix and create a pop band. We hated what we stood for, and we didn't know how to manipulate the situation to bend it in our favor except to do the best we could on the first record, [with the hope] we could start to create something organic [afterward]. On the second record, that's what we've done.

Despite the band's best efforts, *O2* did not sell as many copies as O-Town's first album. In late 2003, the band was dropped by its record label. Fans immediately circulated ***petitions*** in the hopes of getting O-Town signed to a new record label, but these efforts were unsuccessful.

The boys of O-Town eventually made the decision to ***disband*** and go their separate ways. Several band members, including Ashley Parker Angel, Trevor Penick, and Erik-Michael Estrada, launched solo music careers. Jacob Underwood and Dan Miller went on to join new bands and participate in other music projects. Ashley Parker Angel commented on the experience and the breakup several years later in an interview with the *San Francisco Chronicle*:

> We left on great terms. We broke up just because there was no way for O-Town to get ahead. We were the last band to squeeze through the boy-band window, and the way we came together and the nature of the contracts we had to sign were so horrible. I support what [the other guys are] doing. They support what I'm doing. I don't feel bad.

2

Making Da Band

Pleased with the success of *Making the Band*, MTV executives decided to keep the show going without O-Town. The network reinvented the franchise by signing Diddy, one of the world's best-known hip-hop *moguls*, to head up the show as executive producer. MTV hoped the change would give *Making the Band* a more distinct hip-hop flavor and bring in viewers who did not watch the original show.

MTV programming executive John Miller released a statement explaining why the network wanted Diddy to be involved in the new edition of *Making the Band*:

> Once we committed to a new season of "Making the Band," the first person who came to mind was P. Diddy. He's a star maker who has created and produced numerous #1 musical acts. He is the perfect person to take "Making the Band" to the next level.

WHO IS DIDDY?

Diddy, formerly known as Puff Daddy and then P. Diddy, is a rapper and record producer. Born Sean John Combs on November 4, 1969, he

Sean "Diddy" Combs is a Grammy Award-winning rapper. He's had great success producing albums for other performers, such as the rapper Notorious B.I.G. and singers Mary J. Blige and Jennifer Lopez.

grew up in a New York suburb just north of Harlem.

Diddy studied business administration at Howard University before accepting an *internship* at a New York record label known as Uptown Records. In two short years, Diddy went from intern to vice president at Uptown Records. Though he was eventually fired from the job, he managed to get enough money together to start his own record label.

Diddy's label, Bad Boy Records, signed several up-and-coming musical acts, including rappers Notorious B.I.G. and Craig Mack. Around this same time, Diddy also began to make a name for himself as a record producer and rapper. He has produced albums for Aretha Franklin, Mariah Carey, Mary J. Blige, Usher, and TLC. In 1997, he released *No Way Out*, his first solo album as a performer.

Shortly afterward, Diddy decided to expand his empire into other industries. He began his own fashion line, which he called Sean John. He also appeared in several films, including *Made* and *Monster's Ball*.

Given all of his previous success, many people wondered why Diddy wanted to take the helm of *Making the Band.* "I have been creating stars since I was 19," he explained, "and this show will give insight into what it takes to be at the top. I'm excited to be working with MTV and doing what I love to do—create and nurture new talent."

MAKING THE BAND 2: SEASON ONE

The new edition of *Making the Band,* also known as *Making the Band 2,* started out much like the first. Thousands of people showed up at the national open-call to audition for the show. The network chose 50 aspiring rappers, singers, and musicians out of the lot and flew them to New York to meet Diddy.

Diddy and other representatives from Bad Boy Records watched the 50 hopefuls perform before choosing 15 finalists to be part of Diddy's "boot camp." The finalists were moved into a luxury townhouse on Manhattan's Upper West Side, where they practiced writing and performing songs.

Nearly 50,000 people auditioned for *Making the Band 2.*

Diddy warned the finalists that not all of them would make it to the end. His goal, he said, was to select only the best of the best to be part of a new hip-hop/R&B group. Diddy eliminated several cast members from the show as the season progressed. During the last episode of *Making the Band 2*'s first season, the group's lineup was chosen. Band members included Sara Stokes, Dylan "Dilinjah" John, Rodney "Chopper City" Hill, Lynese "Babs Bunny" Wiley, Lloyd "Ness" Mathis, and Fredrick "Freddy P" Watson.

SEASON TWO

The second season of *Making the Band 2* premiered on MTV on June 18, 2003. The show featured the chosen band members from season one: Sara, Dylan, Rodney, Babs, Ness, and Freddy. Together, they decided to name themselves Da Band.

Bad Boy Records

Bad Boy Records was founded by Sean "Diddy" Combs in the early 1990s. It began as a small record label. The first musical acts to sign contracts with Bad Boy were Christopher Wallace (Notorious B.I.G.) and Craig Mack. Both performers followed Diddy from Uptown Records after he was fired for being difficult to work with.

The first record released under the Bad Boy label was Notorious B.I.G.'s *Ready to Die*. Craig Mack's debut album, *Project: Funk Da World*, was released shortly afterward. Both albums sold very well and received good reviews from critics. Bad Boy went on to release many other commercially successful albums from acts like Total, Faith Evans, 112, and Diddy himself.

In September 2009, Diddy signed a new deal with Universal Music Group's Interscope Records. Under the terms of the deal, Interscope will distribute all of the music created by artists who sign with Bad Boy in the future.

Diddy (back, center) poses with the six members of Da Band. They were picked from the 15 finalists who had begun the season on *Making the Band 2*.

Diddy sent the members of Da Band on several missions at the beginning of the season. In the first episode, they were forced to walk from Manhattan to Brooklyn to buy a cheesecake for Diddy. They were also asked to wash cars, read aloud a biography of Russell Simmons, and memorize lyrics to some of Diddy's favorite hip-hop songs.

In the third episode, Diddy informed the band members that they would have six weeks to write and record their first album. After experiencing some early difficulties, the group eventually came together to complete the task.

Da Band's first album, *Too Hot for T.V.*, was released in September 2003. Popular singles included "Tonight" and "Bad Boy This Bad Boy

Members of Da Band pose backstage at MTV's Times Square Studios in New York, September 2003. That month, the group's first album, *Too Hot for T.V.*, was released by Diddy's Bad Boy Records.

That." The album went gold—meaning it sold at least 500,000 copies, as certified by the Recording Industry Association of America (RIAA). While impressive, the 600,000 units of *Too Hot for T.V.* that were purchased fell below Diddy's expectations.

SEASON THREE: TROUBLES BREW

The third season of *Making the Band 2* premiered on MTV on March 4, 2004. The first episode followed members of Da Band as they celebrated the release of their album and prepared to begin a demanding concert tour. But the band was far from being a happy family. Members began fighting with each other almost immediately.

The first argument involved Sara, who wanted to skip a concert to return home to see her mother. Her bandmates, particularly Chopper City, didn't want her to

Fast Fact

Diddy served as a producer on *Run's House*, an MTV reality show that followed rapper Reverend Run and his family.

go. Sara missed the concert but eventually returned and made up with the group. Dylan also upset the other members of the band as well as Diddy by missing concerts, radio show appearances, and other important events.

When Dylan finally returned, Diddy held a meeting with Da Band. He talked about throwing Dylan out of the group. Unfortunately, the threat didn't seem to have much impact on Dylan's behavior. He continued to miss concerts and other planned appearances as the season progressed. Diddy became frustrated with Dylan's attitude and with the overall progress of band. He complained that Da Band's concert performances were "lackluster." To help the group improve, Diddy shared a few of the tricks he'd learned over the years.

In addition to honing their stage performance, the members of Da Band also began work on their second album. Unfortunately, they had a hard time agreeing on the songs they should be recording. Diddy became dissatisfied with their efforts and insisted that they work harder.

THE END OF DA BAND

During the final episode of *Making the Band 2*, Diddy finally had enough of Dylan's irresponsible behavior. He kicked Dylan out of Da Band and asked him to leave the house. The other members of the group went home for a short vacation. But when it was time for them to return to

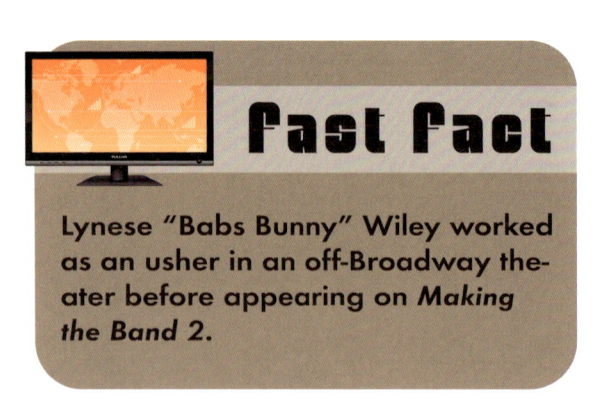

meet with Diddy, none of them showed up.

Diddy became angry. When he met with Da Band a couple days later, he announced his decision to dismantle the group. Diddy tells the band members they've blown a great opportunity—and shown everyone in the world what not to do when trying to launch a music career.

The news that Da Band was done came as a surprise. However, several of the band members, including Sara, Chopper City, and Freddy P, express a desire to move on to something else. Diddy also tells Ness and Babs Bunny that he believes they have talent and will continue to work with them if they are interested in pursuing solo careers.

After leaving Da Band, Sara, Chopper City, Freddy P, Ness, and Babs Bunny continued to make music on their own. Chopper City, who now performs under the name Young City, appeared on the soundtrack to the movie *Hustle & Flow*. He also put out an album on the Bad Boy South record label, but never achieved great commercial success. Ness, who now performs under the name E. Ness, has put out several mixtapes but has not recorded an actual album.

3

Making Danity Kane

Although Da Band's implosion ended *Making the Band 2* after three seasons, there was no denying that the show's formula worked. MTV renewed the franchise and invited Diddy back to head the show. This time, he decided to put together an all-girl group.

Auditions for *Making the Band 3* took place in the fall of 2005. The *Making the Band 3* casting-call notice that appeared on Backstage.com, a site that lists audition notices, read:

> **Seeking—Rockin' Girls: ages 18+, no-nonsense, hardworking, talented individuals who can respect each other's differences and achieve success as a group, singers and vocalists who play instruments are welcome, but no instruments will be provided.**

Young women from all over the country traveled to Los Angeles, Miami, and New York City to audition for *Making the Band 3*. Many of the hopeful contestants were excited to have the chance to work with Diddy. Others were just looking for an opportunity to launch their music careers any way they could.

SEASON ONE

After scouring several cities for potential music stars, Diddy chose 19 finalists to move into a New York City loft and appear on *Making the Band 3*. His goal was to find performers who had it all: the right look, dancing ability, and a great voice.

Fast Fact

Approximately 10,000 young women auditioned to be in the first season of *Making the Band 3*.

At the end of the third episode, Diddy asked four of the finalists to leave the show. Leslie was sent home because Diddy feared her attitude and desire for a solo career would cause trouble in the group. Tyra, Celeste, and Paschun were sent home because they couldn't dance as well as the rest of the cast.

Other girls—including Lavantae, Patti, Roxanne, Erika, Kristen, Leche, and Bethany—were also sent home as the season progressed because their dancing and performing was not up to Diddy's standards. In the last episode of the first season, Diddy asked only three girls to return for the second season: Aundrea, Aubrey, and Malika.

SEASON TWO

Season one of *Making the Band 3* was ranked as the number one show in its time slot among viewers between the ages of 12 and 34. Many viewers were eager to see who else Diddy would choose to join Aundrea, Aubrey, and Malika in the competition to form an all-girl supergroup. Nationwide auditions were held in May and June of 2005. Thirty-eight finalists were chosen to go to New York City. Diddy picked 18 of the 38 to move into a house with Aundrea, Aubrey, and Malika.

The new girls of *Making the Band 3* spent some time getting to know

Making the Band 3 finalists Dominique, Wanita, and Aundrea practice vocals and choreography during the filming of the MTV reality show's second season in New York, August 2005.

the old girls before being sent to Times Square to sing and raise money for charity. Diddy cut seven of the girls from the show early in the season because he was displeased with their singing or dancing ability. Malika, one of only three veterans from the first season of *Making the Band 3*, was among the seven girls asked to leave.

As the season progressed, Diddy cut several more girls from the show until only 11 remained. These girls were split into two groups. The first group, named SHE (She Has Everything), included Aubrey,

Aundrea Fimbres, Dawn Richard, Wanita "D. Woods" Woodgett, Aubrey O'Day, and Shannon Bex perform on MTV's *Total Request Live*. The five singers survived the cuts on *Making the Band* to form the all-girl group Danity Kane.

Denosh, Jasmine, Kelli, and Melissa. The second group, named Chain 6, included Aundrea, Dawn, Dominique, Shannon, Taquita, and Wanita. The two groups were asked to sing at a Backstreet Boys concert. SHE was booed off the stage when two of the girls began singing off key. But Chain 6 did well enough to make the crowd cheer.

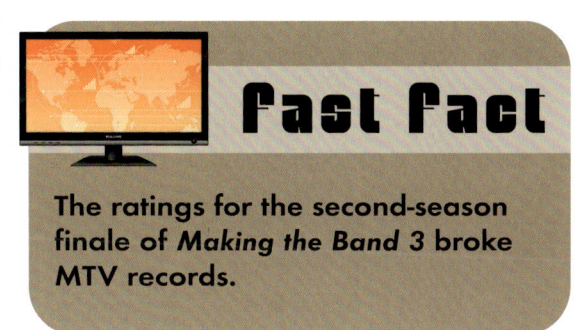

Fast Fact

The ratings for the second-season finale of *Making the Band 3* broke MTV records.

In the final episode of season two, Diddy chose five girls to be in the band. The five were Aundrea Fimbres, Aubrey O'Day, Dawn Richard, Shannon Bex, and Wanita "D. Woods" Woodgett.

SEASON THREE

The third season of *Making the Band 3* premiered on MTV on June 15, 2006. The girls begin the huge task of officially launching their music career as a group. They performed together in public for the first time during NBA All-Star Weekend in Houston, Texas. Neither the crowd nor Diddy was pleased with the performance. Afterward, the girls tried to improve by taking voice and dance lessons.

During the fifth episode of the season, Diddy finally gave the girls his approval and told them that it was time to begin recording their first album. The girls decided to name their band Danity Kane. They worked hard in the recording studio and created several new songs. By the end of the season, their album was finished and ready to be released.

In the final episode of *Making the Band 3*, viewers were treated to a performance by Danity Kane. The girls performed four songs from their self-titled debut album, including their first single, "Show Stopper."

THE RISE AND FALL OF DANITY KANE

Danity Kane's debut album was officially released on August 22, 2006. The album sold more than 90,000 copies during the first day and more than 230,000 copies in its first week. It even outsold other highly await-ed albums that were released the same week, including Paris Hilton's debut album and Outkast's sixth album, *Idlewild*.

Danity Kane's first single off the album, "Show Stopper," was incred-ibly popular. It was one of the highest debuts of 2006 on the Billboard Top 100. Only two days after its release, the song had become the sec-ond most popular download on iTunes. By November 2006, Danity Kane's album was certified platinum by the RIAA—meaning it had sold a million copies.

the Danity Kane Manga

Danity Kane band member Dawn Richard has always been a fan of comic books. She frequently drew her own comics while recording songs in the studio. One day, Diddy spotted a character Dawn had drawn. He asked Dawn what the character was called. Dawn told him the character's name was Danity Kane.

That character inspired the name of the band. It also inspired a Danity Kane series of comic books. The series featured a superheroine who could control the world with her voice. The first comic book in the series was released September 29, 2008.

In early 2010, Dawn Richard announced that she would be creat-ing a manga adaptation of the Danity Kane comic book for release in the spring. The old comic book series was inspired by the music scene in modern society. The new Danity Kane manga takes a slightly different direction. It focuses on a young girl who has been sent from a distant planet to help bring peace to her people.

Despite this success, rumors about a Danity Kane breakup began to surface less than a year later, as reports circulated that a couple band members wanted to focus on solo careers. But other band members tried to lay the rumors to rest by posting messages on their personal Web sites and MySpace pages. Dawn Richard wrote:

> **To answer all the rumors that's been out there about Aubrey and D. Woods pursuing their solo careers. We support them in their decision. However, myself, Aundrea and Shannon are choosing to continue in our efforts to make Danity Kane the best for our fans who love us and what we represent AND the respect we have for our group.**

Danity Kane singer Aubrey O'Day has been involved in several projects outside the band. She won a role in the Broadway musical *Hairspray* in 2008, and appeared in the film *American High School* in 2009. In 2010, she began filming another reality show for MTV.

Aubrey O'Day also denied the rumors through a personal message to fans that was posted on her MySpace page. Her message read:

> Once again I would like to put to rest absurd rumors. I love being a member of Danity Kane and have always been down with DK musically. I'm looking forward to a second DK album and I totally support all members of DK in all of their endeavors.

Danity Kane released its second album, *Welcome to the Dollhouse*, on March 18, 2008. The album sold 236,192 copies in its first week. Less than one month later, it was certified gold by the RIAA.

The first single from *Welcome to the Dollhouse* was "Damaged." Chosen by fans to be the album's first single, it was Danity Kane's most successful song. The digital version was downloaded by more than 5 million people. The video was also very popular, ranking number two on MTV's list of the 25 most-viewed music videos of 2008.

These successes didn't insulate Danity Kane from internal problems. Aubrey and D. Woods left the band in 2008. Although it was rumored that the remaining three members of the group would record a third album, Dawn Richard confirmed that Danity Kane was officially broken up during an interview with MTV News on January 28, 2009.

4

Making Day26 and Donnie Klang

After the mega success of *Making the Band 3*'s all-girl group Danity Kane, Diddy returned to MTV once again for *Making the Band 4*. This time, he decided to put together an all-male group. Auditions were held in Los Angeles, Houston, Orlando, Atlanta, Chicago, Detroit, and New York City. The casting-call notice that went out through Backstage.com made it clear that Diddy was not looking for rappers or MCs this time. He wanted singers and dancers with "voices rivaling Justin Timberlake and moves rivaling Usher on the dance floor."

MAKING THE BAND 4: SEASON ONE

Making the Band 4 premiered on MTV on June 18, 2007. One of the season's first episodes featured an elimination round involving nearly 60 contestants. Diddy picked the 20 performers he liked best and asked the other contestants to leave the show. The chosen 20 moved into a New York City house to live together and compete for five spots in a new band.

After a performance at New York City's B.B. King Blues Club, four more contestants were eliminated. But their places didn't stay empty for long. Diddy brought in 11 more singers to join the show's 16 remaining contestants and announced that all 27 men would compete against each other in a sing-off. Twenty of the performers were chosen to move on.

Diddy continued to eliminate contestants throughout the season until only 10 remained: Donnie, Michael, Jeremy, Brian C, Robert, Qwanell, Willie, Brian A, DeAngelo, and Dyshon. In the season finale of *Making the Band 4*, Diddy made a surprising announcement: he would not be deciding which of the 10 finalists would be in the new band. Instead, he would leave the choice up to MTV viewers. Viewers were invited to vote for their favorite band members online throughout the month of August.

The winners of the viewer vote were announced in a special live event on MTV on August 26, 2007. Donnie Klang, who received the most votes, was offered a solo artist contract on the Bad Boy label. Five others—Brian Andrews, Mike McCluney, Qwanell "Q" Mosley, Robert Curry, and Willie Taylor—were chosen to be in the band. During the live show, Diddy also announced that there would be a second season of *Making the Band 4*.

SEASON TWO: THE DAWN OF DAY26

The second season of *Making the Band 4* premiered on MTV on January 28, 2008. The five band members, who had decided to call themselves Day26 in honor of the date that their band was officially formed, reunited with Donnie Klang in New York during the first episode. Diddy surprised them by announcing that his all-girl band Danity Kane would be joining the boys in the house. In a battle of the sexes, the two groups would go head to head to see which could finish recording their album first.

Danity Kane performed well at the beginning of the competition. Having recorded one album already, the girls felt more confident in the

Donnie Klang performs during the *Making The Band 4* season finale show. Before appearing on *Making the Band 4*, the singer from New York had auditioned unsuccessfully for *American Idol*.

Making The Band 4 winners Robert Curry, Brian Andrews, Qwanell Mosley, Willie Taylor, and Michael McCluney celebrate together on the show. The five performers formed the group Day26.

studio than did the boys. Things were going so badly for the boys that Diddy ordered them to stop recording and get more vocal training. After a lot of hard work, however, Day26 got the okay to go back to the studio and begin recording once more.

The girls of Danity Kane won the competition, finishing their album a day before the boys of Day26 finished recording theirs. For his part, Donnie Klang was unable to get his album completed before the end of the season, though he did record quite a few songs. All of the *Making the Band 4* participants celebrated their accomplishments with Diddy in the final episode.

Day26's self-titled debut album was released on March 25, 2008. The album reached number one on the Billboard 200 chart and sold more than 190,000 copies in its first week. However, it did not perform nearly as well as Danity Kane's second album. The boys of Day26 knew that the pressure was on. They needed to prove that they

Fast Fact

Danity Kane's second album, *Welcome to the Dollhouse*, was recorded in only five weeks.

could hold the interest of fans when they were not on TV. In an interview with *Jet* magazine, Willie Taylor said that he and his bandmates were eager to show the world that they were more than just reality TV stars:

> A lot of people say you can get lost behind the fact that we're a reality-show group and that's not the case. We like to look at ourselves like we're just a group that happened to meet on TV and the world was able to watch us get together. We have love for each other like any other group would and probably more. We're looking to when the MTB4 logo is dead, buried and just a memory, that Day26 is carrying on.

SEASON THREE: TOURING AND TROUBLES

Willie, Brian, Mike, Qwanell, and Robert got the opportunity to prove that Day26 was a legitimate musical act in the third season of *Making the Band 4.* This season of the show followed the boys as they went on a nationwide tour with Danity Kane and Donnie Klang. The tour was meant to promote both groups' current albums as well as Donnie Klang's upcoming album, titled *Just a Rolling Stone*, which was scheduled to be released on September 2, 2008.

Diddy kept a close eye on all of the performers as they prepared for their shows. He pushed them to practice as much as they could before the Making the Band 4 Tour started. After three weeks of hard work,

Danity Kane, Day26, and Donnie Klang hit the road to perform in front of millions of fans and TV viewers. All of them did extremely well on stage the first night, and they got even better as the tour went on.

Unfortunately, the magic didn't last for everyone. Diddy met with Danity Kane during the end of the first part of season three. He had noticed that the girls were having trouble getting along, and he'd heard the rumors of a breakup. Several of the girls admitted that they were having difficulty communicating with their bandmates. Aubrey blamed Diddy and Bad Boy for many of Danity Kane's problems.

After listening to what everyone had to say, Diddy decided that Aubrey and D. Woods needed to be cut from the band. He then told the

Cheri Dennis

Cheri Dennis never appeared on *Making the Band 4*, but the singer was part of the Making the Band 4 Tour. She also recorded "Ooh La La," the theme song for *Making the Band 3*.

Born in Cleveland, Ohio, in 1979, Cheri grew up singing in a church choir. For as long as she can remember, her dream was to become a singing star. She moved to New York shortly after leaving high school. Within two weeks, she met Diddy at a party. Seizing the opportunity, Cheri started singing for him. He was so impressed with her talent that he signed her to his record company, Bad Boy Records.

Cheri made several guest appearances on albums recorded by other Bad Boy artists, including Mase, Faith Evans, Notorious B.I.G., Diddy, and Danity Kane. She also released her own album, *In and Out of Love*, in 2007.

The members of Danity Kane and Day26 pose together backstage after an appearance on MTV's *Total Request Live*, February 2008. The third season of *Making the Band 4* showed how the two groups interacted while on tour.

remaining members of the band—Aundrea, Shannon, and Dawn—that it was up to them to decide whether or not Danity Kane had a future.

SEASON THREE, CONTINUED

The second part of the third season of *Making the Band 4* premiered on MTV on February 12, 2009. This part of the season followed Day26's efforts to record a second album. The show also featured Donnie Klang, who was promoting his first album, and the remaining members of Danity Kane as they discussed the future of the group.

Fast Fact

Day26 won Best Group honors at the 2009 BET Awards.

TV viewers were glued to the show as they watched all of the drama unfold. The boys of Day26 were having trouble getting along. They fought about everything from creative differences to money troubles. Donnie Klang was also having difficulties with his career, and he worried that Diddy would drop him from the label if his album sales didn't improve. The girls of Danity Kane had their own drama as they tried to move forward in their careers.

In the season finale, Diddy told the girls of Danity Kane that they would be released from their contracts. Dawn stayed with the label, but said she was disappointed about the demise of the band. Donnie Klang eventually resolved the issues he had with his own career and began writing songs for his second album. The boys of Day26 also

Fast Fact

Donnie Klang's debut album, *Just a Rolling Stone*, peaked at number 19 on the Billboard 200 chart.

overcame their problems and released their second album, *Forever in a Day*, on April 14, 2009. The album debuted at number two on the Billboard 200 and sold more than 113,000 copies in its first week.

5

Making Diddy's Other Shows

aking the Band isn't the only reality show Diddy is involved in. The hip-hop mogul also worked as an executive producer on two other popular shows: *Making His Band* and *I Want to Work for Diddy*. *Making His Band* aired on the MTV network. *I Want to Work for Diddy* aired on VH1.

MAKING HIS BAND

Diddy mentored musicians and created stars in *Making the Band 2*, *Making the Band 3*, and *Making the Band 4*. In 2009, he decided to make the experience more personal. He created *Making His Band*, a show that auditioned singers, drummers, guitarists, bassists, and keyboardists. The competitors who made it though the grueling auditions were promised a very special prize: they would become part of a backup band and join Diddy on stage for his next tour.

More than 40 competitors were chosen to appear on the show. They moved to Los Angeles, where they lived together in a large house and competed for a spot in the band. Diddy called on five judges to help him decide who would make the final cut. The judges included Laurie

Ann Gibson, a choreographer who had worked on past seasons of *Making the Band*; Om'Mas Keith, a composer and music producer; Romeo Johnson, a vocal coach; Rob Lewis, a music producer and songwriter; and Nisan Stewart, a musician and producer.

Throughout the season, the contestants were challenged to begin learning and performing songs from Diddy's upcoming album, *Last Train to Paris*. Diddy stopped by occasionally to see how the contestants were progressing. The judges cut everyone who didn't perform to Diddy's standards or who fell short in the judges' own eyes.

The season finale of *Making His Band* aired on MTV on October 10. The final 18 competitors were flown to New York City to perform one last time and find out who would be in Diddy's backup band. The finalists included vocalists, keyboardists, guitarists, bass players, and drummers. Of the 18, only seven winners were chosen. The winners included Jaila, Maureen, and Meghan on vocals; Brockett and Jason on keyboards; Chris and Mike on drums; and Jamareo on bass.

WHO WANTS TO WORK FOR DIDDY?

In 2008, Diddy decided that he needed a new personal assistant—a person to help him with everyday tasks. He used traditional recruitment methods to fill the position, but had little luck. That was when he decided to create a competition-style TV series to find the perfect person to assist him in his day-to-day activities.

The series, which was named *I Want to Work for Diddy*, was scheduled to appear on VH1 in the summer of 2008. Diddy launched the show by conducting a nationwide search for people who were looking for new job opportunities. Thousands applied, but only 13 finalists were chosen to appear on the show.

On *Making His Band*, Diddy and his associates auditioned singers, drummers, guitarists, bassists, and keyboardists. Ultimately, a team of talented musicians was formed to accompany the rapper on his Last Train To Paris Tour.

The finalists included Suzanne Siegel, a crime reporter from New York; Mike Barber, a banker from New York; Stefanie Sitzer, a student from California; Kim "Poprah" Kearney, an *entrepreneur* from Georgia; Boris Kuperman, a legal assistant from Virginia; Kendra Haffony, a sales assistant from New Jersey; Redouane Tadjer, a club promoter from Massachusetts; Laverne Cox, a hostess from New York; Brianna Davis, an administrative assistant from Texas; Deon Sams, an executive assistant from California; Rob Smith, an Iraq war veteran; Georgette Cardenas, a mortgage broker from Florida; and Andrew Long, a personal trainer from California.

Each episode of *I Want to Work for Diddy* pitted contestants against each other in a series of challenges. Nearly all of the challenges were based on the real-life experiences of the personal assistants who had worked for Diddy in the past. At the end of each challenge, contestants

Diddy (left) and Phil Robinson (right) are pictured with Bad Boy Records singer Cassie. Phil Robinson had worked as Diddy's manager before taking the position as a judge on *I Want to Work for Diddy* in 2008.

faced a panel of judges that determined who stayed and who would be cut from the show. The panel of judges was made up of Kevin Liles, executive vice president of Warner Music Group; Bad Boy executive Phil Robinson; and former Diddy assistant Capricorn Clark.

At the beginning of the season, contestants were split into two teams: the Uptown Team and the Downtown Team. The teams competed against each other in challenges during the first eight episodes. The challenges included completing a long list of tasks, finding a model for a Sean John print ad, assisting Diddy's family, and selling perfume. At the end of each show, one contestant was eliminated and escorted from the building by Diddy's security guards.

When only four contestants remained, the format of the show was changed from a team competition to an individual competition. When only three remained, Diddy interviewed each candidate. Ultimately he chose Suzanne Siegel, the crime reporter from New York, to be his personal assistant.

I WANT TO WORK FOR DIDDY 2

MTV was pleased with the success of the first season of *I Want to Work for Diddy*. In April of 2009, the network announced that it would be renewing the show. Casting began for *I Want to Work for Diddy 2* within the week. The casting-call notice posted on Backstage.com read:

> **Seeking—Participants: males and females, must be 21 or older by June, must have a "whatever it takes" attitude, big personality that stands out amongst the other candidates, available and on-call 24/7 and cater to Bad Boy Chairman, P. Diddy, characters welcome.**

I Want to Work for Diddy 2 premiered on MTV on November 2, 2009. Out of the thousands who auditioned for the show, only 11 were selected for the job competition. The lucky 11 included Ebony Jones, a high school algebra teacher from Texas; Daniel Orrison, a wine steward from Maryland; Ivory Tabb, a public relations specialist from New Jersey; Dalen Spratt, a business owner from Texas; Jennifer Bauer, a model from Michigan; Melissa LeEllen, an executive assistant from New York; Kennis Bell, a public relations student from Texas; Blake Sunshine, a talent promoter from Massachusetts; John Bonavia, a mall manager from Washington D.C.; Zach Wright, an Internet manager from New Jersey; and Noelle Johnson, a pageant queen from Michigan.

As in the first season, the competitors had to impress Diddy to be given the *coveted* assistant title. They also had to impress a panel of judges that included Bad Boy executive Phil Robinson, entrepreneur Andre Harrell, and former Diddy assistant Capricorn Clark.

All of the show's contestants lived together in Manhattan, but once again, they were split into two teams. Each episode featured the teams competing in a variety of challenges. They were asked to shoot a print ad for the new Sean John logo, collect donations for charity, assist Diddy with press reviews, and work in Diddy's recording studio. At least one contestant was eliminated in each episode.

Kim "Poprah" Kearney, one of the contestants on the first season of *I Want to Work for Diddy*, made a special appearance in the second episode of *I Want to Work for Diddy 2*. She rejoined the competition but eventually revealed that she only did so as a spy for Diddy. After making the revelation, Poprah served as an elimination judge.

The teams competed with each other until the sixth episode. At this point, the format of the show was once again changed to individual competition. Contestants continued to get eliminated afterward until only two—Daniel and Ebony—remained. Their final challenge was to report to Bad Boy headquarters and personally assist Diddy with a listening party for the company's employees. They were also required to make a presentation explaining why they wanted to work for Diddy. Although both contestants did well, Diddy chose Ebony as the winner of *I Want to Work for Diddy 2*.

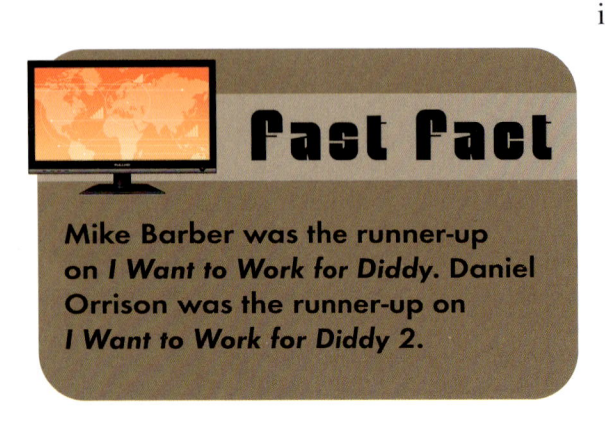

Fast Fact

Mike Barber was the runner-up on *I Want to Work for Diddy*. Daniel Orrison was the runner-up on *I Want to Work for Diddy 2*.

Diddy was born in the Harlem neighborhood of New York City. In 2010, the hip-hop entrepreneur announced that he wanted to open a business school in Harlem.

DIDDY'S FUTURE PLANS

Given the broad range of his interests and accomplishments, it's impossible to predict everything Diddy may decide to undertake in the future. One new field he has decided to enter, however, is education. In February 2010, Diddy announced plans to open up his own New York City business school in Harlem.

"I want to have an academy that's known for building leaders," he told CNN. "I feel that's one of the things I can have an impact on. I try to lead by example. I try to show people that there's no excuse, especially young people, that if I can do it, then you can do it."

Chronology

1999 The opening audition for the first season of *Making the Band* is held on November 6.

2000 The first season of *Making the Band* debuts on March 25.

2001 O-Town releases its debut album on January 23.

2003 *Making the Band 2* premieres on MTV on October 19; Da Band releases its first album on September 30.

2005 The first season of *Making the Band 3* premieres on MTV on March 3.

2006 Danity Kane's self-titled debut album is released on August 22.

2007 The first season of *Making the Band 4* premieres on MTV on June 18.

2008 Day26 releases its self-titled debut album on March 25; season one of *I Want to Work for Diddy* begins on August 4; Donnie Klang releases his first album, *Just a Rolling Stone*, on September 2.

2009 *Making His Band* debuts on MTV on July 27.

2010 On February 1, Diddy announces his intention to open a business academy in Harlem.

Glossary

aviation—a field that involves the development, design, and operation of airplanes and other aircraft.

coveted—highly desired.

disband—to break up.

entrepreneur—a person who creates and manages his or her own business.

executive producer—an individual who supervises the production, distribution, and promotion of an entertainment project.

genre—a style or category, especially of art or entertainment.

internship—a temporary position that provides students and new professionals with supervised job experience.

manga—a comic drawn in a style created in Japan in the late 1900s.

mogul—a powerful or influential businessperson.

petitions—formal, written documents that are signed by multiple people to request a change.

Resources

FURTHER READING

Helsby, Wendy. *Teaching Reality TV*. Auteur Publishing: Leighton Buzzard, 2010.

Huff, Richard M. *Reality Television*. Santa Barbara, CA: Praeger Publishers, 2006.

Ouellette, Laurie. *Reality TV: Remaking Television Culture*. New York: NYU Press, 2008.

Wittman, Kelly. *Sean "Diddy" Combs*. Broomall: Mason Crest Publishers, 2007.

INTERNET RESOURCES

http://www.mtv.com

The official MTV Web site offers full episodes of MTV shows in addition to photos, cast bios, episode summaries, and message boards.

http://www.vh1.com

The official VH1 Web site offers full episodes of VH1 shows, show clips, bonus clips, episode summaries, and more.

http://www.day26online.com

The official Day26 Web site offers information about the band as well as photos, videos, and tour information.

http://www.danitykane.com

The official Danity Kane Web site provides information about the band in addition to videos and an online community for fans.

Numbers in **bold italics** refer to captions.

KAREN SCHWEITZER is an author and education writer. She has written numerous articles for magazines, newspapers, and Web sites like About.com. She has also authored ten nonfiction books for young adults, including biographies of Shaun White, Tyra Banks, Sheryl Swoopes, and Soulja Boy Tell 'Em. Karen lives in Michigan with her husband. You can learn more about her at www.karenschweitzer.com.